IMAGES OF
Tyneside

Evening
Chronicle

IMAGES OF
Tyneside

breedon **books**
PUBLISHING

First published in Great Britain by
The Breedon Books Publishing Company Limited
44 Friar Gate, Derby, DE1 1DA.
1995

To purchase copies of these archive photographs
telephone the Newcastle Chronicle & Journal, Photosales Department
on 0191 2016001 to request an order form.

ISBN 1 85983 005 6

Printed and bound by Butler & Tanner, Frome, Somerset.
Cover printed by Lawrence-Allen, Avon, Somerset.

Contents

Introduction

TYNESIDE and the region around it is an area of startling contrast. It lies at the heart of the ancient kingdom of Northumbria, a land where the echoes of history can still be heard loud and clear.

It was here that the Romans settled, building the mighty Hadrian's Wall from coast to coast. It was here that the Saxons recognised the might of the Tyne and Wear as defences against their enemies and it was here that the Normans came, saw, conquered and built the castle from which Newcastle takes its name.

To the north, east and west lie lush lowlands and bleak, often blood-soaked border country – the high and forbidding Northern Pennines.

The Tyne, though, has dominated the region for centuries, The Romans, Normans and Saxons all left their mark. Later came the coal industry, and with it iron-making and ship-building.

From the ancient Newcastle, Tyneside spread towards the North Sea on either banks, its anthem the song of hammer on metal as for more than 100 years it built some of the mightiest and proudest ships afloat.

There is history here around almost every corner. From the grandeur of Durham Cathedral to the humble simplicity of the Ven Bede's Saxon church at Jarrow, from the tumbling clear streams of the dales and fells to the awesome majesty of rivers like the Tyne and Wear.

This selection of pictures, taken from the unrivalled photographic library of the *Evening Chronicle*, sets out to tell the story of Tyneside and the lands around it, and especially the story of its people who have, for centuries, been its greatest asset.

In good times and bad they have been indomitable.

Echoes of the Past

Newcastle's Groat Market in the early 1800s in an engraving by T.Hodgetts.

The panorama of the Tyne looking down river and taken in 1968. Redevelopment has changed the scene drastically and has included complete facelifts for both sides of the river.

The grandeur of the Tyne Bridge from Swan House looking towards Gateshead. Beneath the bridge, on the Gateshead bank, is the floating night club *Tuxedo Princess*.

A view little changed over the years, even though it is dated 1929. It shows the Tyne Bridge from beneath, from Queen Street, Newcastle. The picture was taken to illustrate one of the many suicide deaths the bridge was to know.

A very early print of Old New Bridge Street, Newcastle, showing the Church of the Divine Unity which stood there. The area where the tower stood is now the site of the city's Laing Art Gallery.

Newcastle Maternity Hospital in Edwardian days. The building, in New Bridge Street, was later used as a centre for the unemployed and later radio and TV studios for the BBC.

Newcastle's historic Guildhall and Exchange in 1829. The open colonnade to the east of the building was then used as a fish market. In 1880 it was bricked in and converted into an annex for the Exchange.

Northumberland Street, Tyneside's premier shopping area, in a pre-World War One picture. The top-hatted groom on the coach and two is obviously waiting for a customer who is very much 'the carriage trade'.

A clutter of trams and trolley-buses in Newcastle's Northumberland Street in November 1938.

Northumberland Street in 1910. The white sign in the centre advertises the Queen's Hall for sale, freehold, and suitable for use as an hotel, warehouse or picture house. In fact the building was to become the now-closed and demolished Queen's Cinema.

Northumberland Street, Newcastle, in 1958. Even then there were worries about the health effects of exhaust pollution.

Percy Street, in Newcastle city centre, in 1952.

A turn of the century picture of Nelson Street, Newcastle, with the Caledonian Railway offices and the Gaiety Theatre on the left.

Nun Street, Newcastle, in 1957, then dominated by the Farnons store, split on either side of the street.

Bainbridge's, Newcastle's oldest department store, in 1952. In 1976 the store moved from its site to Eldon Square Shopping Complex. Later Binn's – to become part of the House of Fraser group – took over the building. In 1995 they, too, closed their store.

The Scandinavian Sailors'
Home, in Westmorland Road,
Newcastle, where a new
extension was opened in April
1931.

Grey's Monument, in the
heart of Newcastle, in 1904.

Newcastle's Royal Arcade in tones of light and shade in 1948. It was later dismantled with a view to rebuilding after redevelopment of the site. Eventually a replica was built.

Pilgrim Street, Newcastle in 1926, before demolition to make way for the building of the Tyne Bridge.

Pilgrim Street, Newcastle,
pictured around 1882.

Newgate Street,
Newcastle, in 1910,
with the long-gone
Empire theatre in the
middle picture (left).

Newgate Street, Newcastle, in 1951. Old open-ended double deckers were still the norm.

Newcastle's Central Station in pre-World War One days. St Nicholas' Cathedral is seen in the background while the transport of the day was evidently horse-drawn cab or tramcar.

An impression of Newcastle's Central Station as architect John Dobson originally planned it. The portico was built to a much smaller scale yet the station was still reckoned one of the grandest in the country.

St Peter's Church, Oxford Street, Newcastle, rapidly disappearing under the demolition men's hammers in August 1936.

Ye Olde Lord Collingwood Inn, in Pudding Chare, Newcastle, in the 1920s. The building is now a garage for *Evening Chronicle* vehicles.

George Stephenson in all his glory. The statue stands in Westgate Road, Newcastle, opposite the site of the old *Evening Chronicle* offices.

Westgate Road and Collingwood Street, Newcastle, in 1957. Note the lengthy queue for trolley-buses on the far left winding around the statue of George Stephenson.

Westgate Hall, on Westgate Road, Newcastle. A handcart is one of a handful of vehicles on the move in October 1951.

The old *Newcastle Chronicle* office on Westgate Road, Newcastle, in 1961, shortly before the move to a new building in nearby Groat Market.

Newcastle's famous Literary and Philosophical Society building on Westgate Road in 1971.

It might not be a greenfield site but for these youngsters in Kent Street, Shieldfield, the back lane of their terraced houses was their playground in the early 1960s.

Washing day at Noble Street, Newcastle, in 1955, in the days when tumble dryers were undreamed of luxury.

Life in the gutter for youngsters in Elswick East Terrace, Newcastle, in March 1959.

Prospect Place, Newcastle, and a typical back street scene in September 1959.

Life in the back streets might look grim but there was time for a laugh in 1971 in Shumac Street, due for demolition and where some residents had lived for more than 50 years.

Lord's it isn't but the magic of cricket still wove its spell in a Newcastle back street in 1962.

Newcastle's Sandgate as it was in the last century and then the centre for most of the city's keelmen, shipwrights and seamen.

A fall of snow transforms Barras Bridge, Newcastle, and St Thomas' Church in the centre background, in December 1935.

The gardens of the Black Gate, Newcastle, in May 1953.

The timeless charm of the arch of the Black Gate, part of the remains of Newcastle's Norman fortifications.

The Black Gate, Newcastle, in the nineteenth century, and business in the corner shops nearby is obviously slack.

The Heber Tower, on Newcastle's West Walls, used as a wheelwright's workshop in 1903.

Going down. Part of the £750,000 demolition scheme to clear Newcastle's Byker area for redevelopment early in the 1980s.

A tranquil Newcastle scene in April 1926 – but already the warning signs are up at the Armstrong Bridge, unable to bear the strain of heavy traffic which was diverted to the steep gradient on the right.

The Armstrong Bridge, across Jesmond Dene, Newcastle, in 1926. The speed limit, because of the frailty, was 5 mph.

A panoramic view of Newcastle taken from the steeple of St George's Church, Jesmond, down Osborne Road.

Jesmond Station, Newcastle, in October 1949, when the suburban station's gardens won a British Railways prize.

Another view over the rooftops of Jesmond in April 1967. The area is a favourite with students.

Lake Lodge, at Gosforth Park, Gosforth, looking like a gingerbread cottage in 1977 when, after restoration, it was the home of the warden of the 140 acre Gosforth Park Nature Reserve.

Gosforth High Street in the days of the horse-drawn tram.

Trade and Industry

One of the earliest shops in the
London & Newcastle Supply Stores
chain in Whitley Bay in the 1920s.

Balmbra's in Cloth Market, Newcastle, at the turn
of the century, then still known as the Wheatsheaf
pub before fire destroyed the façade.

An unidentified Tyneside grocery shop sometime early in the century.

A pre-World War One picture showing that industrial disputes were nothing new. Outside a Newcastle newsagent's the poster (bottom left) reads: 'Are postmen underpaid?

Mutton at 5d a pound and best beef at 7d, that was the cost of meat in 1902 when this picture of Gilroy's shop in Churchill Street, Newcastle, was taken.

F.Beavan, in Shields Road, Newcastle, in 1954. It had just been acquired by Great Universal Stores.

Talking turkey in the Grainger Market, Newcastle, in December 1936.

April 1956 and a Newcastle fish and chip shop where customers were coming to terms with a price increase – fish slices nine 'old pennies' and chips 6d.

Milk roundsmen in Jarrow in the early 1900s.

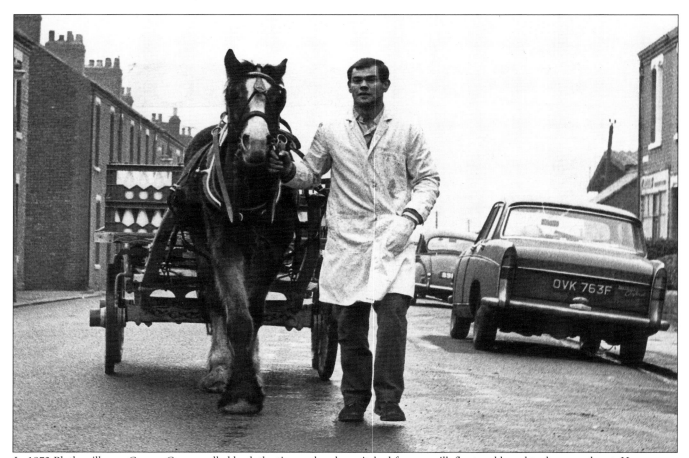

In 1972 Blyth milkman George Cowen rolled back the times when he switched from a milk float and bought a horse and cart. He preferred the company, he said.

Newcastle telephone exchange in February 1947 when it was logging up to half a million calls each day.

Wright's Biscuits factory in South Shields in November 1951, when automation still needed a helping hand.

The Go Gay Shoe works, started in a little converted snack bar in South Shields after World War Two, was looking around the world for markets when this picture was taken in 1965. The firm had just won an order, the first ever, from Fiji.

Vickers, Scotswood, in 1946. Steam roller production had taken over from arms manufacturing. An early example of The Peace Dividend.

The S.Jennings cycle works at Morpeth in the 1910s.

The main roadway on the Tyne Bridge was rapidly placed in position during its construction.

Construction work on the Tyne Bridge in 1928.

The super tanker *World Unicorn* dominated the terraced houses of Wallsend as she neared completion in 1973.

The giant crane at the Walker Naval Yard pictured in 1949 and reputed to be the largest of its type in the world.

One of the most famous landmarks on the Tyne for many years, the cableways of Palmer's Shipyard in Jarrow. They were demolished in 1938.

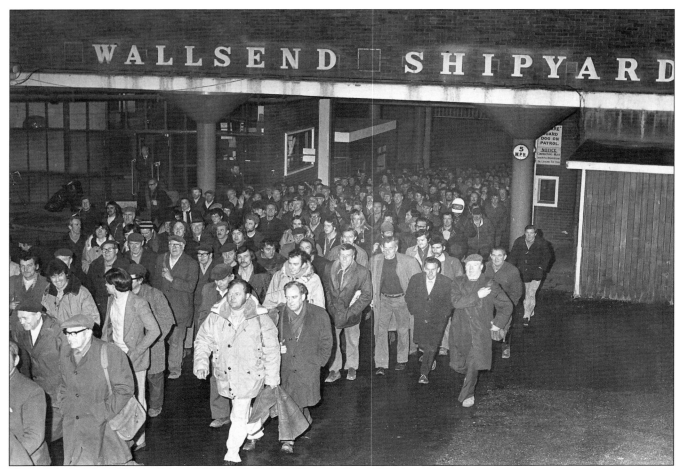

The rush home. Swan Hunter Shipyard, Wallsend, in 1977. The yard is now closed.

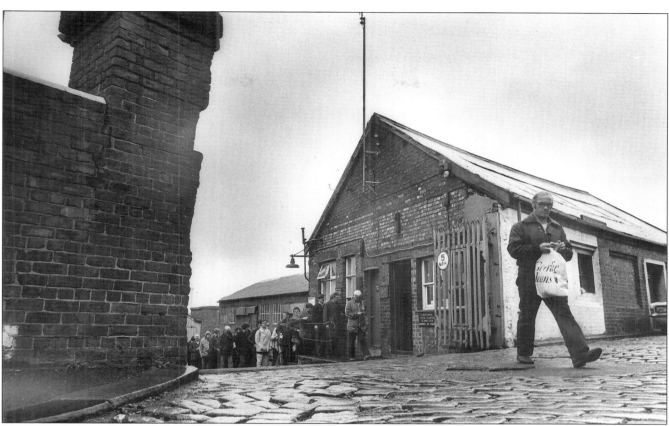

The Redheads shipyard at South Shields in 1982. The yard had just been scheduled for closure. It was pay day when the news was announced.

Linton Colliery, Ashington, with miners going down for the last shift before closure.

His last day at the pit. A lone miner walks home on the day Burradon pit closed in May 1982. It was the oldest pit in Northumberland.

Pit ponies Bullet, Darkie and Baldie, with pitmen George Oxley, William Armstrong and Bob Cowell, at the Marley Hill Pit near Gateshead in 1983, shortly before the mine's closure.

Getting Around

Out for a gentle ride in the 1880s in the Tyneside village of Swalwell.

Yes, but which way is forward? This tricycle made for four was once the pride of Newcastle shopkeeper Mr W.H.Carr, who had a store in Grainger Street. The photograph dates from 1870.

A rare picture of the pioneer members of the Novocastrian Cycling Club in 1891. The scene includes the club's only lady member.

A long and hard road waits ahead for vintage cycle enthusiasts Jack Henderson and George Hepple in April 1952 when they set out from Newcastle's Haymarket for Morpeth on an annual Good Friday run.

A 'Ladies Only' tram carrying munitions workers along Scotswood Road, Newcastle, in 1917. This was a lunchtime trip with two cars coupled to form a tram train to cope with the numbers.

The last tram in Tynemouth on its final journey from New Quay, North Shields, to Whitley Bay in August 1931.

Entertainer George Robey was aboard this decorated tram which toured Newcastle in 1931 raising cash for the
Cancer Campaign.

Crowds off to the races at Gosforth by tram from Central Station, Newcastle, in June 1947.

On the scrap heap. Gateshead Tram Depot in Sunderland Road in 1951 as vehicles await dismantling after buses have ousted them from their routes.

A Newcastle Blue Bus on service on the Gosforth to Central Station route in February 1931.

A United bus on the Ashington to Newbiggin run in days of oil lamps and solid tyres. Pictured in 1920.

Showing just how far they could go, a new bus design is demonstrated at Northern Coachbuilders of Cramlington in April 1938. In fact it went to 38 degrees.

The first of a fleet of new Leyland buses in operation in December 1948. These are employees from C.A.O.Parson's works going home for lunch. It was thought by transport chiefs that many more would opt for a home lunchbreak thanks to improved services.

Ready for the racegoers, buses line up in West Clayton Street, Newcastle, ready for the trip to Gosforth Park in 1952.

Trolley-buses, lorries, vans and cars all added up to city centre congestion in Newcastle in 1955.

In 1936 rail electrification came to the Newcastle-South Shields line. Workmen are seen here preparing for the switch from steam to electric at the crossing from Newcastle to Gateshead. The Tyne Bridge, in mist, can be seen in the background.

Days gone by and all travellers had to show their tickets before boarding a train. These barriers and ticket offices were newly-installed in June 1937.

Any seats left, do you think? A northbound express enters a packed Central Station in Newcastle in July 1951.

The grandeur of steam, but this picture was taken to highlight the new lamps installed (right upper) at Newcastle Central Station in 1958.

Central Station, Newcastle, on a more than usually busy November night in 1962. A bus strike left commuters queuing up for the then electrified British Railways trains to the coast.

A rare picture of the barge used for civic occasions, festivals and for the surveys of the River Tyne some time in the last century.

Even in 1929, when this picture was taken, they were asking whether 'a bridge or tube railway' would replace the Tyne ferries. Seen here, on a rare meeting, are the vehicle-carrying boat the Tynemouth and the North Shields
passenger-only ferry.

The Tyne ferry *Wallsend* more than paid for herself by serving faithfully for more than 60 years on the Hebburn and Wallsend run. Here she is seen in May 1949, shortly before retirement.

One of the few
remaining cable-
operated ferry boats
in the North-East was
at Blyth. Two cyclists
and a solitary car
make their stately way
aboard in 1930.

Not seen here as the
most ladylike of vessels,
the Shields ferry belches
black smoke in
December 1959 as she
prepared to cross the
river from south to
north.

In July 1954 the ferry *Collingwood* plied its last trip between North and South Shields. She was fondly known as 'Ha'Penny Dodger'.

The ferry boat *Tynemouth*, an early roll-on-roll-off boat with a full load of lorries, cars and a Land Rover in 1962.

The Hebburn ferry the *Tyne Princess* ploughing the waters of the river in January 1975.

A flight of fancy at Cramlington Aerodrome at a gala day in July 1930. The vehicle in the foreground is the Whickham & District Ambulance.

Tyneside Folk

The glory days for the Commercial Exchange in the Quayside Guildhall in Newcastle. In 1901 it would be packed each day with dealers, coal owners and shipping merchants.

Emerson Muschamp Bainbridge, founder of the Bainbridge department stores in 1838. By the turn of the century the company could boast over one and a half miles of showrooms around the country.

Catherine Cookson at the age of 19 and (inset) a more modern 'Wor Kate'; South Tyneside author Catherine Cookson, one of the world's most successful writers.

Brian Redhead, Tyneside born and educated, and later to become one of Britain's best-known broadcasters, especially as anchorman in Radio Four's *Today* programme.

T.Dan Smith, in the 1960s 'Mr Newcastle' and the man who, as council leader, helped transform the city. He was later disgraced and jailed for corruption.

Gateshead's
Olympic
runner
Brendan Foster,
atop a position
he occupied so
often in a long
and
distinguished
career on the
track.

(Left) Where local folk met. A rare picture of one of Tyneside's more unusual markets, the Dog Market, which was held on the roadway of St Andrew's Street, off Clayton Street. The scene is undated but was probably taken at the turn of the century. (Right) A North-East postman in his distinctive uniform (and obligatory horn) from the second half of the last century.

A fine body of men. The staff of Pelaw Railway Station in the 1890s.

Two candidates for confirmation
in Elswick, Newcastle, in 1885.

Foremen from the Armstrong Whitworth
Newcastle works in their Sunday best on their
annual outing at the turn of the century.

When the milk
came fresh from
the cow. A
Tyneside Victorian
street milk seller
with her measure
at the ready, and
under the watchful
eye of the law.

Beating the
bounds, and
collecting cash
along the way, in
Newbiggin in May
1931.

A departure by train from Newcastle in May 1931 marked the start of a very special day for North Shields fishwife Polly Dankin, who was to receive a brooch from the Prince of Wales for her work for the Royal National Lifeboat Institution.

In 1936 this balloon seller was doing a roaring trade in the centre of Newcastle.

How Tynesiders lived – or would like to have lived? The latest in cosy living on display at the Royal Show, held on the Town Moor, Newcastle, in 1956.

Newcastle West Rotary Club and their families on a Sunday afternoon trip down the Tyne aboard one of the river's ferries during the 1950s.

(Left) Chips – with plenty of salt and vinegar! Still a firm favourite in November 1962 when these two lads out on the town stopped off for a bite at a Newcastle fish shop for the traditional 'paper'. (Right) A fixture outside South Gosforth Station for more than 30 years when this picture was taken in 1967, the Finley Fish Barrow. Lily Scott, whose mother started the business 70 years before, is at work as usual.

The 'Hoy Dot' on Tyneside and still an old tradition observed in the North-East in 1972. The groom would throw small change to local youngsters as he left for the wedding.

For generations girls in their last term at Newcastle's Church High School flung their uniform bonnets into the Tyne. The tradition died in 1973 when the hated headgear was phased out.

One of Newcastle's oldest traditions died, victim of local government reorganisation, in 1974 when the offices of Sheriff, Under Sheriff and Town Clerk disappeared. Each year they met the city's Freemen. Seen here are (left to right) Mr R.K.Dotchin, chairman of the Freemen, Lord Mayor Alderman A.Gray, Dr C.Lipman, Sheriff, and Alderman C.McKeag, Under Sheriff.

Time to Celebrate

Lifeboat Day in Newcastle at the turn of the century when boaters and bonnets were just the thing for a sunny day – except, that is, for the Newcastle firemen taking pride of place in the parade.

Civic dignitaries on the first electric tram in Newcastle. The lady at the controls is the Mayoress of the city.

Empire Day on Tyneside in 1903, captured by one of the earliest pioneers of photography Charles MacLeod, who, as well as being Vicar of Mitford, Northumberland, was also a very accomplished camerman.

A royal visit to Alnwick in 1906 following King Edward VII's opening of the bridge named after him in Newcastle. The bridge took rail traffic across the Tyne.

It was party time in Elswick, Newcastle, and there was plenty to celebrate. The year was 1918 and the end of World War One was the best of reasons to let your hair down.

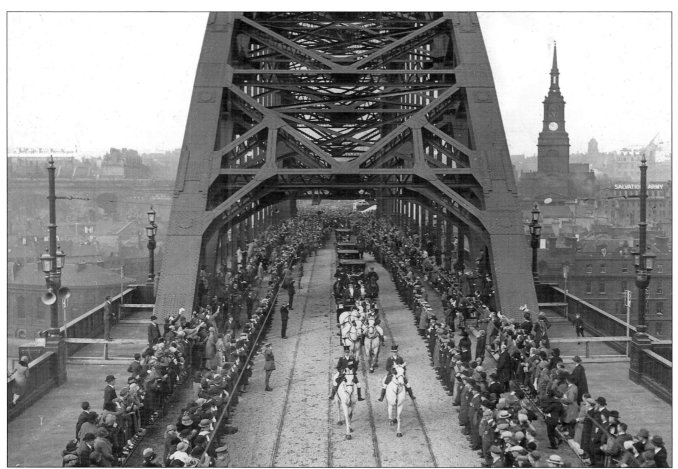

The royal procession carrying King George V passing the newly-opened Tyne Bridge in 1928.

The splendour of the North-East Coast Exhibition, held on the Town Moor, Newcastle, in 1929. None of the buildings in the picture remain, but the lake in what is now Exhibition Park is still popular for boating.

Shipbuilders Conference delegates taking time off at the North-East Coast Exhibition of 1929, held on the Town Moor, Newcastle. Here they are admiring the statue of 'Spring'.

The Prince of Wales, later to become King Edward VIII, saw the effects of the Depression on the North-East for himself in 1929. Here he is visiting a Tyneside pit village.

A decorated Newcastle tram in 1932, decked out to raise cash for the Newcastle Eye Hospital Extension Fund appeal.

A street party in full swing at Mill Street, off Scotswood Road, Newcastle, in September 1933.

They were hanging out the bunting in Northumberland Street, Newcastle, in May 1935 to celebrate the Silver Jubilee of King George V.

John Dobson's superb portico at Newcastle Central Station in May 1937 with the bunting hung to celebrate the Coronation of King George VI hiding some of the accumulated grime of decades.

Riding the Bounds at Morpeth in April 1952. The Mayor, Councillor W.W.Mitchell, is flanked by the traditional halberd bearers.

Pine Street, Newcastle, was not going to be outdone by its neighbours when it came to Coronation decorations. The date is 30 May 1953.

Decorated trolley-bus and petrol-bus, spruced up for the coming Coronation celebrations, being inspected by Alderman William McKeag, Lord of Mayor of Newcastle, in May 1953.

The *Evening Chronicle* and sister paper *The Journal* helped make the welcome warm when these Tynemouth crowds turned out for a visit by the Queen in October 1954.

The Mayor of Gateshead, Councillor B.N.Young, welcomed Queen Elizabeth to Gateshead for her tour on Tyneside in October 1954.

"We took the bus from Balmbra's and it was heavily laden." They did the same 100 years later, in 1962, for the centenary anniversary of Blaydon Races.

The Lord Mayor's coach and four, plus police horses, passing Newcastle's Central Station in August 1967.

Teaching and Healing

These bright-eyed youngsters were the apple of their teachers' eyes when this picture was taken at Longbenton National School in 1902. They had won the accolade of never having been absent from class.

Wardley Colliery School, Felling, in 1928.

Story time in Byker parish hall, Newcastle, in the early 1940s.

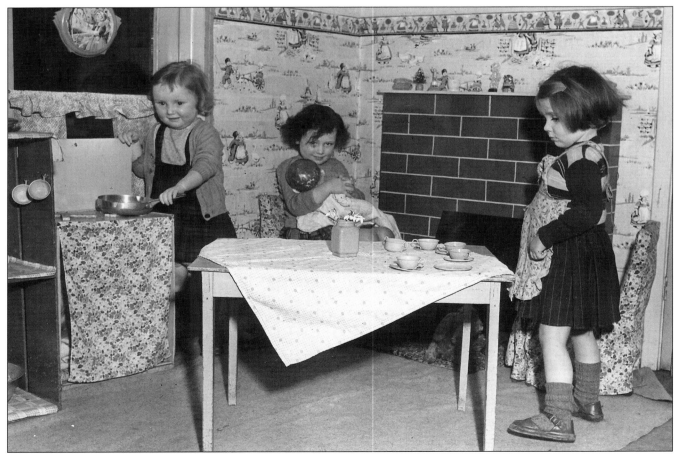

Nursery teaching in Newcastle. The date is 1952.

Two pre-school youngsters in Newcastle slums in 1971. This emotive picture was used in a Shelter housing campaign to highlight the problem.

New extensions to the Newcastle Eye Hospital near Barras Bridge, were opened by the Duchess of Northumberland in October 1933.

The Fleming Memorial Hospital for Children in Newcastle in 1961.

A Political View

Some of the 200 men from Jarrow who took part in the march on London in October 1936.

Paddy the stray black mongrel became mascot of the Jarrow Marchers in October 1936. He is pictured here with local MP Ellen Wilkinson, who proved a firebrand in the 1930s and 1940s.

The speakers at the Northumberland Miners' Picnic at Bedlington in June 1955, with the procession of banners led by Leader of the Opposition, Clement Attlee, second from left.

Big Day in Durham – the Miners' Gala in 1957 when pit banners and bands paraded through the city before the annual gathering of pitmen at the Racecourse.

A younger Michael Foot, second left, was guest speaker at the Northumberland Miners' Picnic in 1960.

Prime Minister Harold Wilson (left) and Jim Callaghan at the Durham Miners' Gala in 1965.

Labour leader Hugh Gaitskell waves to the crowds on Durham Miners' Gala Day in July 1961.

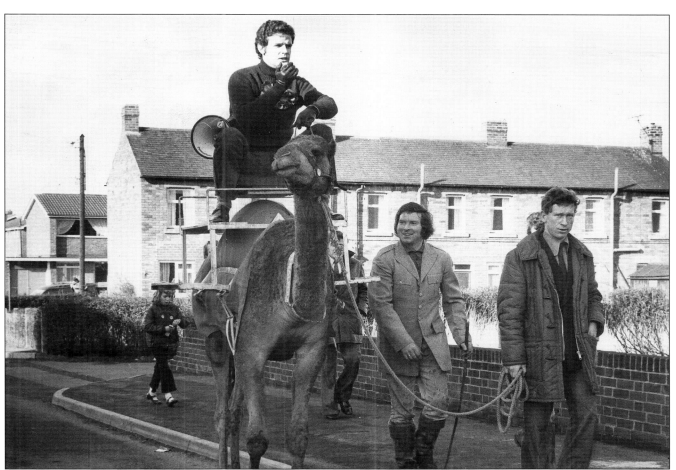

But will the voters get the hump? Neil Balfour's election campaign for Chester-le-Street in 1974 saw him hitting the road Lawrence of Arabia style. His rival, Labour's Giles Radice, won the seat hands down to nobody's surprise. A planned confrontation between the two was upset when the camel refused to ride in a horsebox to their meeting.

Would-be local councillor at Brandon, Co Durham, Ernest Brown, used horse power to pull the voters out in 1976. What Dolly the horse thought about it we shall never know.

Dr David Owen finds canvassing
face-to-face just how he likes it,
no holds barred. Here he is on the
receiving end of an argument put
by an Iranian student in
Northumberland Street,
Newcastle, in 1983.

Former United States President Jimmy Carter
boards the Lord Mayor's coach during his visit
to Newcastle in 1987. The trip was memorable
for his Geordie rendition of 'Howay the lads'.

Tyneside at War

September 1939 and a group of Tyneside children and their mothers prepare for evacuations. Many were billeted in the Lake District.

Knitting for the troops in November 1939. Members of the Heaton Social Service Knitting Party hard at work at Park View House, Heaton, Newcastle.

Wartime preparations at the Dental Hospital in Newcastle when students took part in a very different kind of drill – filling sandbags in case of air raids.

In May 1939 recruits for the Army parade at St Thomas' Church, Newcastle.

An essential visit. The scene at the Newcastle Food Control Office early in World War Two as housewives organised their ration cards.

A wartime scene at Hodgkin Park, Newcastle. By November 1940 grass was making way for the plough – and much needed food production.

Gosforth Home Guard step out in style in April 1941.

One of the earliest victims of air-raids was in August 1940 when Trinity Methodist Church, Whitley Bay, suffered badly.

Air-raid damage to houses at Matthew Bank, Newcastle, in December 1941.

The London & North Eastern Railway Goods Station at New Bridge Street, Newcastle, after being hit by German bombs.

Houses, trolley-buses and businesses damaged by a German attack on South Shields, which badly hit the town's Market Place.

South Shields Market Place after the air raid in October 1941.

Bombed out but not beaten, families tuck in to the first hot meal after a Tyneside air raid in April 1941.

Food for the homeless prepared by volunteers after an air raid on Tyneside in October 1941.

After the raid, the reckoning. This was the scene after a German air raid on homes at Matthew Bank, Newcastle, early in 1942.

What could be salvaged lies outside the ruin of homes which suffered in an air raid at St Anthony's, Newcastle, in the spring of 1943.

Rain and Shine

Time to cool off because, for once, the sun is shining. Tynemouth Open Air Swimming Pool in August 1972.

Sun, sea and sand. Who needs the Med? Holiday makers relax on Tynemouth Beach in August 1976.

Four o'clock on a June afternoon in 1954, but more like midnight. A storm-darkened sky meant lighting up time had come very early.

Scotswood, Newcastle, and a damp drive for traffic during flooding in 1975.

November fog in Newgate Street, Newcastle. The year is 1960.

The storms which wrecked the North Pier, Tynemouth, in 1901. More than 300ft of the pier was swept away.

In February 1941 even the war took second place to the sheer problem of getting from 'A' to 'B'. Walking was the only reliable method. This scene is at Barras Bridge, Newcastle.

In March 1953 the bulldozers were called out to keep traffic moving at Denton Bank, Newcastle.

The Tyne ferry ploughing her way through an ice floe during the big freeze of 1963.

Bell's Close, Newburn, in 1970 was more like a polar scene than the Tyne. Here Mr Jim Hooker, of the Tyne Cruising Club, checks to ensure that the mini icebergs are not crushing the moored boats.

It looks like an idyllic scene. Stagshaw Bank, to the west of Newcastle, and a snow plough at work in the winter of 1977.

February 1978 and a stroll down Northumberland Street becomes more like a polar expedition.

The sign says it all. Snow chaos on Old Durham Road, Gateshead, in January 1979.

Fires, Floods and Other Disasters

Flames leapt 40ft as fire engulfed the Appleton's wholesale warehouse and store in New Bridge Street, Newcastle, in September 1956.

Dramatic shots of a fire which engulfed part of Newcastle Central Station in July 1961.

Police officers can only watch as Newcastle Central Station blazes away.

Newcastle Quayside in June 1959 and the roof of a giant dockside shed buckles with the heat from blazing sisal.

Virtually every man and fire-engine available was called out to a huge blaze at Howard's furnishing stores in Clayton Street West, Newcastle, in late December 1953.

High level fire-fighting in Newcastle in August 1960 when the Newcastle brigade was called to tackle a huge blaze at the Northumberland Street store of James Woodhouse and Son.

After the storm the wreckage. The ill-fated vessel was either the *Constance Ellen* or the *Golden Lilly*, which foundered on the Herd Sands at the mouth of the Tyne in November 1893.

Ships that meet, not in the night, but in heavy weather. The 11,400 ton cargo steamer *Georgidore* didn't move far after her launch at South Shields in January 1954. She struck a glancing blow against another ship, the *Hudson Deep*, and then collided with the nearby *Corfield* at the Redhead yard.

Need a hand? South Shields Volunteer Life Brigade were on hand when the *Adelfotis II* ran aground at South Shields in 1963. They rescued the crew by breeches buoy.

The seine boat *Bella* ashore on the rocks at Tynemouth in July 1972. She ran aground in thick fog.

The treacherous Black Midden Rocks at the mouth of the Tyne claimed yet another victim in September 1974 when the Greek-owned *Aliki* ran aground. It was a carbon copy of a disaster which saw another ship meet a similar fate in March the same year.

South Shields ferry landing in February 1978 after the pontoon and superstructure sank. Only the passenger waiting rooms and the watchman's hut escaped total immersion.

In October 1979 the crew of the seine netter *Conduan* were rescued when foul weather smashed her against the rocks at Cullercoats.

In 1900 Cullercoats fishermen found their boats very handy – inland. When the village flooded they were called in to rescue stranded train passengers.

Floodwater at Durham. In September 1975 the River Wear burst its banks and inundated Durham City.

Too good to resist. It was time for a swim when Bensham, Gateshead, became flooded in 1987.

The wind blew harder …and harder, in 1960, blowing down this show marquee at Lambton Park, near Chester-le-Street.

Well, at least it wasn't so stuffy any more. These homes at Park Road, Newcastle, lost their gable ends during storms in 1965.

In 1983 the worthies of Gateshead had a very lucky escape when a stained glass window at the Town Hall blew into the Council Chamber only minutes after a meeting had ended.

The big clean up after it 'rained soapdust' in Gibson Street, Newcastle, after soap dust from the Thomas Hedley factory showered the area in September 1960.

The Morpeth train crash of May 1969 when an Aberdeen-bound express hit the notorious Morpeth curve with fatal results.

A tramcar and bus in collision on the Tyne Bridge in 1947.

Steam and Sail

Sail, steam, and a combination of both, jostle for space at Tyne Dock in 1896.

Newcastle Quayside at the turn of the century with one of the once-familiar 'Puffing' hoppers, which plied up and down the river.

Half enveloped in smoke the Wallsend-built super liner *Maurentania* leaves the Tyne for her first trials at sea in 1907.

One of the dwindling launches from Jarrow by the end of the 1920s was the *Duchess of York*, which went down the slipway in 1928.

'Metal bashing' between the wars at the Swan Hunter and Wigham Richardson yard at Wallsend.

Dredging work at Palmers' Jarrow yard in September 1935, ready for the breaking up of the liner *Olympic*.

Newest of the Royal Navy's battleships, the Walker-built *HMS Nelson* left the Tyne in July 1936. She had a displacement of 33,500 tons and was built at a cost of more than £6 million.

The latest in dredgers in 1951 was the 650 ton motor suction vessel *Bowstar*, seen here on the Tyne after her launch at Willington Quay.

The last trip for the Tyne Customs hailing ship *Orwell* in April 1957. The converted warship which once patrolled the China Seas was declared redundant and towed to Edward Dock, North Shields, for disposal.

Tugs, tramps and the paddle steamer *Dunelm*, off South Shields in July 1952, a typical busy river scene of the day.

Down she goes. *HMS Norfolk* leaves the slipway on the Tyne in 1967.

The Tyne Bridge, dwarfing the minesweeper *HMS Northumbria*, at her moorings in June 1968.

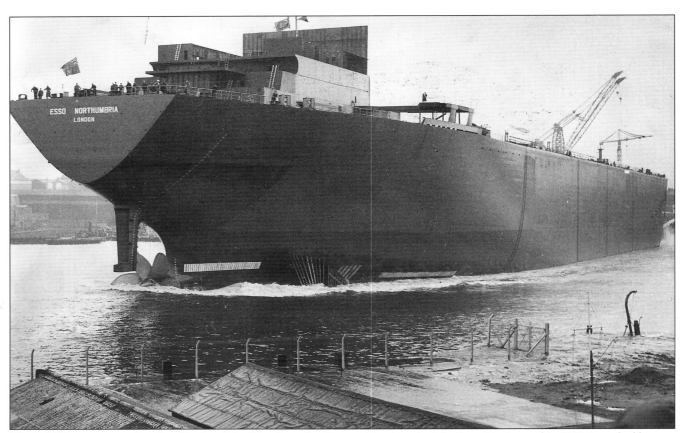

The 250,000 ton super tanker *Esso Northumbria* glides down the slipway at her launch at the Swan Hunter yard in 1969. Launched by Princess Anne, she was then the largest ship to be built in Britain.

The supertanker *Tyne Pride* is nudged from her fitting out position at Wallsend in 1976 to make way for the launch of her sister ship, a 260,000 tonner, whose giant screw half fills the picture.

Entertaining Tyneside

Collecting for the Church, around 1900. The good cause was Annfield Plain Primitive Methodist Church in County Durham.

Elephants parading past the Theatre Royal, Newcastle, in a turn of the century picture.

All dressed up for the big night. In the 1900s tailoring and workroom girls from Newcastle's Fenwick's store donned fancy dress for a ball at the city's Old Assembly Rooms.

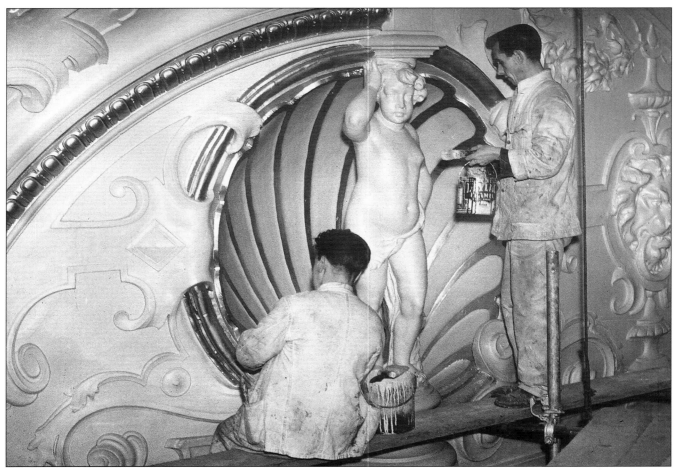

A spot of touching up to the decorations at the Empire Theatre, Newcastle, in March 1950.

First nights are always occasions, and the opening of *The Importance of Being Earnest* at the Odeon Theatre, Newcastle, in 1952, was no exception. Here members of Gateshead's Little Theatre arrive in Edwardian costume.

Rehearsal time at the People's Theatre Newcastle, in September 1953. The play was *Columbe*.

Panto with a glitter. Cinders (June Clair) takes to the Theatre Royal stage in style in the 1953 production of *Cinderella* in Newcastle.

The portico of the Theatre Royal, Newcastle in November 1958, when a good scrub seemed called for to wash away the soot of decades.

Alterations to a cinema in Gosforth in 1960 revealed a treasure trove of old bills and posters.

Balmbra's Music Hall, of Blaydon Races fame, in full swing in January 1964 following the revival of the old music hall to mark the Blaydon Races Centenary Celebrations.

In 1979 Balmbra's, in Cloth Market, Newcastle, could boast the world's only Geordie can-can dancers.

In June 1966, Howard & Wyndham, then owners of Newcastle's 130-year-old Theatre Royal, declared it 'ailing and infirm'. The building still retained its faded splendour though, and is now totally refurbished.

The play's the thing – but not any more in 1971 when these three workmen took a break from demolition to stage the last act at the Jesmond Playhouse, Newcastle.

An undated picture of the then newly-formed Rising Sun Colliery Band outside Buddle School in Wallsend. They were so new that they had not yet been issued with uniforms.

Juvenile jazz bands, a northern tradition, have not always pleased everyone. In June 1974 the Montagu Monarchs, in Newcastle, were staging a counter demonstration against local householders who complained about the noise they were making.

The orchestra in a final rehearsal at the opening of the Paramount cinema in Northumberland Street, Newcastle, in September 1931. The cinema is still open, now as the Odeon.

The Odeon, Northumberland Street, Newcastle, in 1951. Now a multi-screen cinema, the lights are still bright.

Newcastle's oldest cinema, the Olympia in Northumberland Road, in 1960.

In 1972, Rodney Bewes and James Bolam recreated their earlier success when *Whatever Happened to the Likely Lads?* appeared on BBC TV. Bob and Terry drew viewing figures as big as ever in their tale of two Tyneside lads learning to grow up.

Old time dancing – fittingly enough at the Old Assembly Rooms in Newcastle. The long dresses and dark suits style of ballroom dancing began to make a comeback on Tyneside in the 1950s.

Rock around the clock at Wallsend Memorial Hall in 1957. It was claimed to be the North-East's very first rock 'n' roll dance.

Newcastle's Majestic Ballroom in January 1962, and The Twist is all the rage. "It's easy", a 16-year-old told a reporter. Maybe – when you are 16.

Felling's celebrated male voice choir in full voice in June 1951.

Gypsy horse-drawn caravans and steam engines were part of the charm at the Newcastle Hoppings at the turn of the century at Jesmond Vale.

All the fun of the fair. The Town Moor Hoppings funfair in Newcastle in June 1957.

The Newcastle Hoppings funfair, lights blazing in the summer sky in June 1971.

Sporting Tyneside

Chester-le-Street AFC pictured around 1900. When this photograph was published in the newspaper in 1955, several members of the team were still alive and living in the area.

The year is 1900 and Armstrong Brass Foundry footballers are taking part in a fancy dress charity match at Rendall Football Field, Benwell, Newcastle.

In 1930, the whole town seems to have turned out for the annual street football game in Chester-le-Street.

Despite a police ban Chester-le-Street celebrated its traditional Shrove Tuesday street football game, smuggling balls in beneath the noses of the police who were waiting to burst them. The date is February 1932.

Members of the Whickham Cricket Club in 1890s.

Rackets at the ready, members of South Boldon Tennis Club in 1891.

Bathers ready to take a dip in the chilly waters of the North Sea at Roker, Sunderland, at Christmas 1913.

No starting blocks, no designer running shoes and no all-weather track, just sheer grit and determination. These four entrants in a Good Friday running heat held in Newcastle before World War One were all set to race their hearts out for a massive prize of £100.

In 1901 Chester-le-Street, with the River Wear running through it, had a rowing club of national fame. The crew pictured here won the professional handicap event at Durham Regatta.

A regatta at Prior's Haven, Tynemouth, in the early 1900s.

Shooting the river in 1931 as rowers raced for the Joseph Cowen Cup at the Tyne Regatta.

Tynemouth Sailing Club members catching the wind at a meeting in Ryton in November 1951.

Tyneside cyclists take a breather after a day out in Northumberland in 1892.

Only one cycle – and a man's model at that? Percy Park Cycle Club's ladies' day outing in 1896.

A day in the saddle for two Newcastle cyclists at around the turn of the century. They have biked into County Durham. The signpost reads 'Road to Medomsley'.

Bowls on the green at Nun's Moor, Newcastle, in 1909.

(Left) Bill Ward, of Jarrow, bare knuckle champion of Tyne and Wear in the mid-nineteenth century. (Right) Wrestling in St James' Hall, opposite the Newcastle United football ground, was a must for fans of grappling when this picture was taken in November 1957.

Ryton's open-air ice rinks in January 1939. The weather is ideal for a spot of practice by the Newcastle Curling Club.

Whippet racing at an unknown venue on Tyneside in 1920. The owners and punters are almost certainly pitmen at the local mine.

A moment to savour. Newcastle United's FA Cup-winning side enjoy their moment of triumph at Wembley in 1952.

The Geordies are here! Some of the thousands of Newcastle United supporters who headed south to see their team play Arsenal in the 1952 FA Cup Final warm up in Trafalgar Square. United won 1-0 with a goal from Chilean George Robledo.

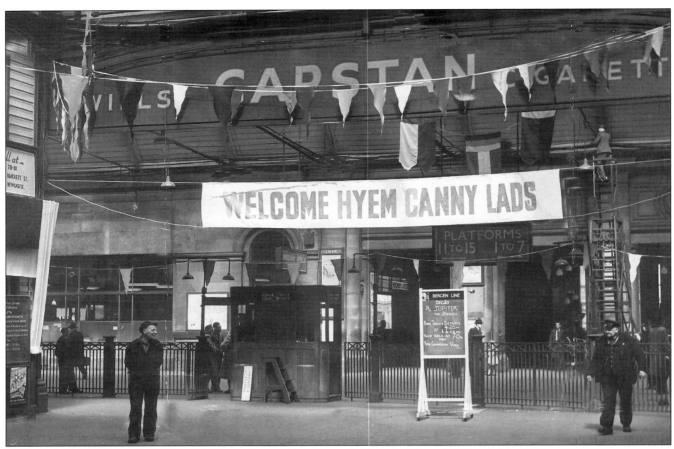

Welcome back to the conquering heroes. The message awaiting Newcastle United at Central Station in May 1952.

May 1952 and the FA Cup comes to Newcastle after the 1-0 win over Arsenal.

'Wor Jackie', hero of Newcastle United, pictured with some of his England caps in 1957.

Down on the Farm

Echoes of a slower way of life on the farm. This rural scene was pictured in September 1950 at Lintzford Farm, on the banks of the Derwent in County Durham.

A race against the weather during harvest time at Brunton Farm, Gosforth, in October 1951.

It might look like just a pile of rubble but in fact these three men were displaying their skills in the art of dry stone-walling at the Royal Show, held on Newcastle's Town Moor in 1956.

Horse shoeing by members of the Royal Army Veterinary Corps at the Royal Show, Town Moor, Newcastle in the summer of 1956.

Potato picking at Avenue Head Farm, Seaton Delaval, in the autumn of 1957.

The show ring at Tynedale auction market, Hexham, in September 1961.

Potato picking at Kirkley Mill Farm, Ponteland, in October 1963.

Not a likely Grand National runner, this Ayrshire bull called William delighted the crowds at the Tyneside Agricultural Show in Corbridge in August 1964.

Sunshine brought the harvest along nicely in September 1956 at Pecks House Farm, Westerhope, Newcastle.

Crawcrook market in December 1975 and the annual poultry sale. Prices had been between 25p and 60p a pound.

Across the Tyne to Gateshead

Gateshead High Street at the turn of the century.

Demolition work in 1926, in preparation for the building of the Tyne Bridge on the Gateshead bank of the Tyne. St Nicholas Cathedral can be seen in the centre of the picture with the Castle Keep to its left.

Bottle Bank, Gateshead, showing all the congestion regularly suffered before the construction of the Tyne Bridge.

Gateshead High Street in 1939. It is traffic free but traders were complaining that shoppers during the day would rather ride into Newcastle than risk crossing the road.

A closure on any one of the bridges across the Tyne has always caused traffic chaos. In July 1951 nothing had changed and when the Redheugh Bridge was closed, traffic, seen here coming off the Gateshead end of the High Level Bridge, was nose to tail for hours.

Gateshead High Street in February 1960, with major work to the railway bridge nearing completion.

Old Durham Road, Gateshead, in 1961. The scene was little changed 30 years later.

The longest escalator in Western Europe. The trip beneath the Tyne via the Tyne Pedestrian Tunnel crossing the river at Jarrow was a long drop for passengers and cyclists. The scene was taken in 1961.

The breakthrough in the construction of the Tyne Tunnel was in June 1966 when, midway under the Tyne, Harry Flynn (left) and Alec Gibson, shook hands.

The skein of railway tracks in mid
picture is Gateshead engine depot, with
the High Level and Tyne Bridges
spanning the river above it. The Civic
Centre tower in Newcastle can be seen in
the extreme upper left of the picture.

Saltwell Towers, in Saltwell Park, Gateshead, a
fairy tale castle in the heart of the town's biggest
park. By the 1970s, though, it was neglected and
structurally unsound.

Cathedral and Castle – Durham City

The majestic loop of the River Wear shows the Cathedral, Castle and old City of Durham.

The grandeur of Durham Cathedral.

Regatta Week in Durham, June 1960.

The Rogation Day procession in Durham in May 1950, with the Cathedral and city in the background.

Around and About

Grange Road, Jarrow, in the 1950s. Little remains today but the old Town Hall with its hanging clock and Christ Church to the left.

The chair of the Venerable Bede in the historic St Paul's Church, Jarrow, in 1933. Legend had it that a splinter from the seat would ensure fertility.

Jarrow town centre from the Town Hall roof in 1954. Redevelopment has completely altered the scene.

Jarrow Slake, now filled in, but once home to migrating sea birds. It was 150 acres of mud, covered at high tide.

Jarrow town centre in 1983.

Going nuts for nuts. Part of the traditional riding of the bounds at Newbiggin included throwing nuts which lead to an inevitable scramble by youngsters. They used to throw raisins, but by 1956 when this picture was taken, that was deemed unhygienic.

Heddon on the Wall Station in 1947 where the flowers won the LNER prize for station gardens. Stooked corn ready for harvesting, fills the field to the right.

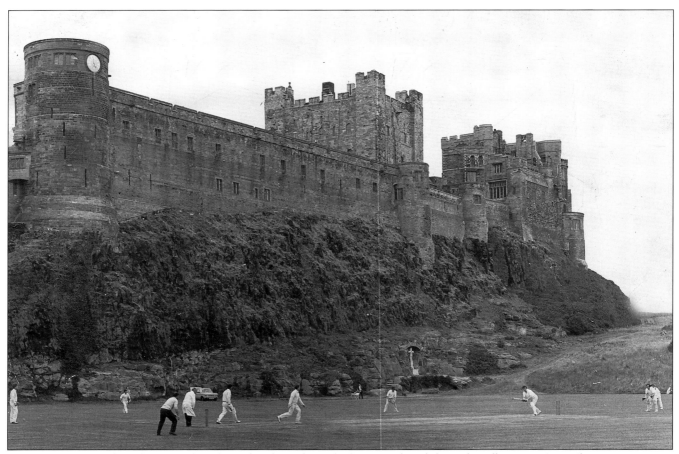

Cricket on the green, but what a grandstand! Bamburgh Castle overlooks a typical English Sunday village scene in April 1974.

Carlisle Park, Morpeth, on a fine May day in 1959.

Alnwick Market Place, virtually traffic-free in 1954.

The glory of north Northumberland. The Harthope burn tumbles over rocky beds at the top of Hedgehope Hill. Nearby is the valley village of Wooler.

The Parish Church of St Cuthbert, Blaydon, in a quiet scene from 1956.

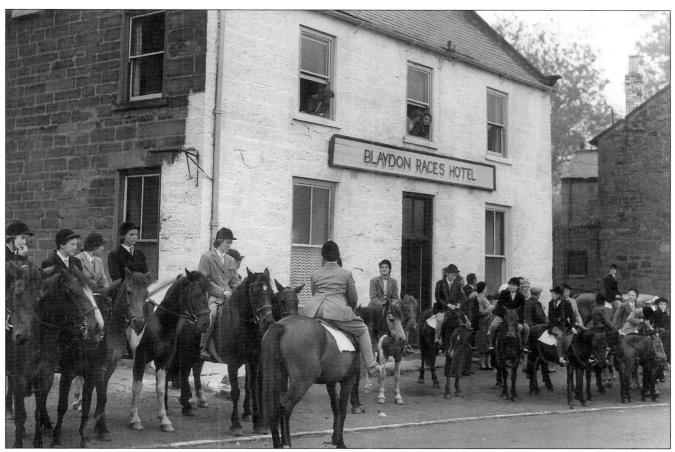

What was once the Stella Straithes Hotel, Blaydon, was by 1959 renamed the Blaydon Races Hotel, after the fact that jockeys in the world-famous event used to stay there.

Ryton village on a quiet day in October 1938.

Baking day at Ryton in the 1890s, with local housewives using the communal oven at Emmaville.

The picturesque charm of the little village of Blanchland, on the Northumberland and Durham border.

Blanchland in 1949. Even the village Post Office is picturesque.

Hexham Abbey on a fine July day in 1934.

Hexham from the air in 1951, showing all the charm of a rural market town.

Hexham Races one Saturday in the 1920s. The racecourse has always been popular as a family venue.

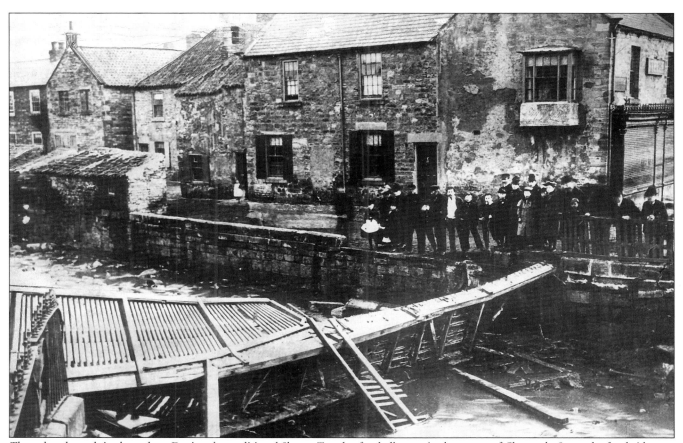

They played rough in those days. During the traditional Shrove Tuesday football game in the streets of Chester-le-Street the footbridge over the River Wear was one of the casualties.

The remote and impressive ruins of Northumberland's Dunstanburgh Castle in May 1973.

Vindolanda, one of Britain's most important Roman remains, during excavations in the early 1970s.

Along the Coast

South Shields Market Place early in the century when riding a tram upstairs was a draughty affair.

A colourful procession in South Shields in December 1937 when the town's Moslems celebrated the Festival of Ramadan. Through its shipping connections with Aden, the town had long been home to a large Yemeni community.

An atmospheric picture of Marsden Beach, South Shields. It could have been taken at any time during the last 50 years. In fact the date is 1986.

North Shields Fish Quay fish wives in their traditional many-tucked skirts in a scene from around 1910.

The monument to Lord Collingwood, architect of one Britain's great naval periods, in North Shields.

Donkeys, sea and sand have always gone together, as they did here at the Long Sands, Tynemouth, in the 1880s.

East Street, Tynemouth, at the turn of the century.

Tynemouth and a seaside scene which could have been captured at any time over the last 100 years. It probably dates back to Edwardian times.

Tynemouth Castle
in 1926, when the
building was still
in the hands of
the War Office.

In 1931, when this picture
was taken, demolition had
just begun of the first
commercial premises in
Tynemouth village, a
barber's shop and pub in
Front Street.

Tynemouth Castle and Haven in calm weather in 1968.

Cullercoats, between Tynemouth and Whitley Bay, a popular alternative to the two seen here in July 1971.

Cullercoats Front Street in the 1890s.

The timeless charm of Cullercoats as seen in 1961.

The links and sands at Whitley Bay at the turn of the century.

Whitley Bay High Street in 1930.

The lights were burning bright in Whitley Bay in 1950 as the town's illuminations were switched on.

Say it with flowers. The flower garden tribute to the 1951 and 1952 FA Cup winners, Newcastle United, courtesy of the council gardeners of Whitley Bay. St Mary's Lighthouse can be seen in the distant centre of the picture.

Whitley Bay Station in 1952, with crowds waiting for the reduced fare electric trains running after 6pm.

Summer at long last. The crowds flocked to Whitley Bay when the sun finally broke through in August 1961.

Storm clouds gather over St Mary's Lighthouse, Whitley Bay, in April 1953.

The Empress Ballroom, Whitley Bay, in April 1954.

Subscribers

Ernest Adamson
Peter Ainsley
John E Alderson
Jeffrey Alexander
Henry Allan
Mrs Ruth Allan
Douglas Anderson
Pamela Margaret Anderson
S Archbold
Craig Armstrong
Robert Armstrong
Miss Sarah L Aspinall
Mrs G Auld
Autoclock Systems Ltd
Jonathan Avanessian
Margaret J Ayers
Margaret Baines
John Banborough
Barbara
Thomas Charnley Barnes
Mr David J Bates
Colin Bell
Doris Bell
Ernie Bell
Mr Thomas Geoffrey Bell
Mrs M Bennett
Dorothy Black
Irene Blain
Vivien Boardman
Ms Christine M Bolam
A H Bottomley
John Boughton
John Boughton
Raymond Richard Bowman
Barry Briggs
M Brittain
Mr George H Brown
Kate Louise Brown
Pat Brown
Mr Charles Buchanan
Mr T W Burleigh
Burlinson Family
Norman Carson
John Hedley Chambers
William R Chappell
Mr Alan Charlton
Mr David Chesser
Mr Frederick Chester
Peter G Coates
Martin & Cate Clarke
Mrs V M Close
Mrs M Genia Collin
J B Collingwood
J G Collingwood
R D Collingwood
Mrs Christina Colledge
Joan Congleton
Robert & Maureen Coombes
Barbara Cox
Margaret Cragg
Mr W G Crampton
John Phillip Crawley
J Creal
Norman Crosby
Margaret & Bob Dale
Michael Dale
Mrs Elaine F Davis
Dr J H Dewar
Jean Sheila Dinnie
Mr James R Dishman
James Ditchburn
David Dodd

Ian A Domoney
E Douglas
E E Douglass
Frederick Hudson Dryden
E Ducas
E M Eastcott
John Elliott
David Paul Evans
Peter Faddy
Stuart James Fair
Mr Thomas Finn
Brian G Flynn
John Forbes
Sylvia Forster (née Corbett)
Sylvia Forster (née Corbett)
Derek Fowers
Michael J Fowler
Vivian Gibbon
Albert Gibson
J J Gibson
P F Gibson
Alan Glover
Mr & Mrs L B Graham
Thomas Graham
Andrew P Grainger
Dr & Mr A C Graves
Mr & Mrs G N Graves
Mr & Mrs H C Graves
Mr & Mrs H L Graves
Malcolm Gray
Malcolm Gray
Alma Doris Greig
Audrey Griffiths
Lillian & Tom Gunn
Keith Gunning
Margaret Caroline Gunton
J Hailes (Management
   Services)
Austin Hall
Mrs Sylvia Hardie
Alexander Hardy
Mr B Harper
Richard Harris
Mrs Edna H Hart
John James Havre
Elspeth Harland
Agnes & Cec Hay
James Heron
Graham Heslop
Mr C Hillary
Ian Hodgson
Kevin J Hogg
Mr Charles Holdsworth
Dr Clive R Hollin
T & N Horner
B H Huddart
Derek Hughes
Niall Andrew Hunter
Mrs Betty Hyde
Irene (1995) from Mam &
   Dad
Carol Ann Irwin
Catherine Jamieson
Michael Jamieson
Brian Jenkinson
Joyce Jenkinson
Mrs E M Johnson
George Johnson
Tom Johnson
T W Johnson
J Joyce
Peter L Kane

Brian Keeller
C Keirl
Theo & Shirley Kelly
David Kennedy
Mrs Kathleen Kessler
John T H Kilpatrick
Robert Kindness
Peter & Pat Knowles
M Lambert
Anne Longstaff
Ken Lumsden
E MacDonald
W H MacDonald
James McDougall
C J McInnes
Frank McKenna
Alan McNeil
Arthur McRae
Mack
Ronald Malone
Geoff Mark (Canada)
Elizabeth Markey
Mr Cyril Marshall
Jack Martin
Derek Carr Mason
Catherine Maughan
Peter Mays
Hazel J Michael
Craig Middleton
Susan Miller
Allan Mitchell
R Monaghan
Florence B Moore
Mr K Morrison
Mrs J S Morton
Mr Raymond Mossom
Mr G M Murphy
George Murray
Laura Jane Murray
Jack & Mary Nattrass
Mr H G Nichol
Carol Noble
Odeon Cinemas Limited
Desmond O'Donnell
Michael Anthony O'Donnell
Mrs Pat Othick
Dorothy Padgett
Eleanor Patterson
Michael Thomas Patterson
Revd Kenneth G Peel
Robert Percy
Mr Victor Percy
Peter & Sheila & Family
George Pickering
Lynne C Potter
Karen Price
David Quinn
James Quinn
Chrystine A C Rae
S C & D A Rand
T H Randall
Mrs Elizabeth Anne Redfern
Gwendoline May Reid
J K & S Reid
Thomas Reid
Frederick Alan Richardson
Mrs Nora Richardson
Brian Ridley
J B Rix
Chloe J Robinson
Jim C Robinson
Mrs Phyllis E Robinson

Colin Rogers
Adrienne Ross
Alan Ross
Neville Henry Ross
Philip H Rowell
Mathew James Rutherford
Mr William Ryan
Mr Kenneth Saunders
Daniel Anthony Savory
Graham Scott
Mr Ian Scott
S Scott
Selby
Alan Sherriff
Mr Michael Shield
Mr Les Slater
Mrs Caroline Smith
Don & Joan Smith
William Alexander Somerville
Arthur H Spence
Frederick Spry
Dorothy Tauba
A W Taylor
Graham Taylor
Sydney Telford
John Thompson
W Thompson
W Thompson
Mr W Thorburn
M Tiffen
S W Tiffen
Kenneth Tollett
Maureen Toward
Maureen Toward
Frank Toward
Paul Tuff
Mr & Mrs G R Turnbull
Mr D Turner
Deryck Tytler
Margaret Walker
Norman Walker
George Sidney Wallace
M Wallace
John J Walton
Mrs N E Walton
Margaret Ward
T W Ward
Theresa Jean Ward
W E Wardhaugh
Thomas Wardle
Mr Phillip Watts
Mr Paul Wears
R S Welsh
Martyn Weston
T G White
John & Kathleen Whiting
G A Wilde
Mr H Wilson
Mr Sydney Wilson
Jack Wiper
Arthur & Winifred Wood
John William Worth
D W Wright
Mr Harry Wright
Margaret Elizabeth Wright
Mr John F Yates
Mr & Mrs T A Yates
June Yeaman
Gary J Young